CW00546848

MUJIB

Bangabandhu Sheikh Mujibur Rahman
Founding Father of Bangladesh

AN INTRODUCTION

Mujib
Bangabandhu Sheikh Mujibur Rahman
Founding Father of Bangladesh
An Introduction

Published in the UK by Nomad Publishing
in cooperation with
Bangladesh High Commission London

Editorial team:
Her Excellency Saida Muna Tasneem
Sabbir Shams & Aninda Rahman
Illustrations by Arafat Karim

The Publishers would like to thank Curious Dhaka and
Charcha Publishers, the designer and printer of the original
Bangladesh version of this book, for their original work,
enabling publication of this international edition.

Email: info@nomad-publishing.com
www.nomad-publishing.com

ISBN: 978-1-914325-14-4
© Nomad Publishing 2022

CIP Data: A catalogue for this book is
available from the British Library

*When you follow in the path of your father,
you learn to walk like him.*

Ashanti Proverb

CONTENTS

FOREWORD

Her Excellency Saida Muna Tasneem
High Commissioner of Bangladesh
in the United Kingdom

FOREWORD

Sheikh Mujibur Rahman was amongst the frontline Afro-Asian civil rights and independence movement leaders who stood alongside global anti-colonisation figures like Mahatma Gandhi and Nelson Mandela in carving out a new future for his people during the turbulent era of decolonisation. He also stands out in a post-partition Indian sub-continent as the founding father of an independent nation state for his people during the turbulent international decolonisation and the emergence of a new world order.

An ever-vigilant guardian of human rights and a champion of the oppressed and marginalised people of Bengal, he built a massive people's platform, standing strong and unyielding against both the last of the British Raj and the post-partition government of Pakistan. Over the course of twenty-four years of erstwhile East Pakistan he led the Bengali people to a freedom movement, culminating in the declaration of Bangladesh independence and the Liberation War of 1971.

Sheikh Mujibur Rahman also laid for Bangladesh the foundation for a secular and inclusive people's republic.

There are very few politicians, dead or alive, who can claim to have accomplished all that Mujib did.

9

He emerged as the undisputed leader and saviour of the Bengali race, motivating 750 million to fight a guerrilla war to liberate Bangladesh. He was also the only Bengali to have earned the title 'Bangabandhu' meaning the 'Friend of Bengal'.

Bangabandhu Sheikh Mujib's legacy is not only one of indomitable struggle for freedom, equality and secularism, but is also an inspiration for new generations.

It is an honour for me to present this book, a tribute to Bangabandhu's life – an opportunity, I hope, for a wider international circle to learn more about this remarkable man whose personal achievements and visions for a secular, progressive and democratic Bangladesh are wrapped up in the very character of the nation state of Bangladesh to this day.

The fact that in recent years, Bangladesh has emerged as one of the fastest growing economies of the world with the strongest credentials in Asia on women empowerment and resilience against the growing threats of climate change, is owed much to its Founding Father and his vision for a 'Golden Bengal'-a vision being relentlessly realised by his daughter Sheikh Hasina.

For that we owe the Bangabandhu an immense debt of gratitude.

Saida Muna Tasneem
High Commissioner of Bangladesh
in the United Kingdom

BANGLADESH
HIGH COMMISSION
LONDON

BANGABANDHU AND VISIONS OF BANGLADESH

Nobel Laureate
Amartya Sen

A Talk to Commemorate the Birth Centenary
of Bangabandhu

Organized by
Bangladesh High Commission, London
in collaboration with the LSE South Asia
Centre, 27 January 2021

"The 75 million people of Bengal will have the freedom to practise their own religions. Secularism does not mean a lack of religion. However, in the last 25 years we have seen religion used as a front for oppression, disrespect and torture. These activities are not allowed in the territory of Bangladesh."

Bangabandhu Sheikh Mujibur Rahman
November 4, 1972

Amartya Sen

In plain Bengali, the word *Bangabandhu* – the term by which Sheikh Mujibur Rahman is uniformly known in his homeland – means 'Friend of Bengal.'

But Sheikh Mujibur Rahman is, of course, incomparably more than that. He was the first great political leader of Bangladesh, the founder of the idea of an independent Bangladesh, the biggest influence on the lives of Bangladeshis and the most admired person in Bengal. And, as has been noted again and again, he can rightly be seen as "the Father of the Bangladeshi nation."

Being a friend of Bangladesh, or *Bangabandhu*, is really an incredibly modest way of describing Mujibur Rahman. The fact that he did not ask for some more grand designation, and that he happily agreed with the term, tells us something really important about the man: he did not seek nominal glory. People admired him instinctively.

I am delighted that the London School of Economics has arranged this occasion and thank the wonderful Director of LSE – we are very grateful, on behalf of all Bengalis anywhere. And the fact that the High Commissioner of Bangladesh also here gives force to what we are going to do in celebration. I am thrilled that I have been given the opportunity to remember him during this celebrations of the centenary of his birth.

Other than paying tribute to this wonderful human being and the great leader that he was, I would also like to say a few words on why his ideas remain so very important in today's world.

Bangabandhu was taken from us. But no one can rob us of the legacy of his clearheaded vision – something that continues to make a real difference to the lives we lead. The subcontinent, including India, I believe, is going through a challenging period of ideological confusion right now, and we have reason to thank Bangabandhu for his guidance as well as his considerable influence. In many distinct ways, Sheikh Mujib's thoughts and analysis have powerful relevance today. Let me choose a short list.

First, Sheikh Mujib was a great exponent of secularism. All countries in the continent, and in particular its largest, India, are in particular need of recalling Bangabandhu's insights on this subject. Bangladesh herself has gone through ups and downs in the history of her secularism. But, since Bangabandhu spoke so very clearly on the kind of Bangladesh he envisaged, we can easily read from his exposition what form he would have liked the nation's secularism to take. I woud like to emphasize here that the association between 'secularism' and 'human freedom' played an inspirational role for Sheikh Mujib. Often in Europe secularism is interpreted as a general hostility to religion with the secular state seen as something that should never tolerate any kind of religious activity. The United States experimented with this kind of secularism at various times. But God and Christianity are so strong in the minds of most Americans that secularism in this form is a non-starter in the USA. In Bangabandhu's thinking secularism did not mean that we should not have the freedom to have religious values. Mujib did not see any great merit in the anti-religious interpretation of a secular state, and he saw no particular point in avoiding religious practice or sacrificing religious freedom in the name of "becoming secular". In November 1972, in Dhaka, as a new secular democracy was being adopted in the Bangladeshi parliament, he spoke widely on what he was specifically seeking in his search to establish the important value of secularism in Bangladesh. To quote from the draft constitution:

> "We will not stop the practice of religion. Muslims will practice their religion, Hindus will practice their religion, Buddhist will practice their religion, Christians will practice their religion. We will only object to the political use of religion."

The importance of religious freedom ranked high. What he sought to stamp out was the political use and indeed political exploitation of religion. It is a view centred on freedom, and with the state not being allowed to interfere in people's practice of their respective religions. Indeed, the state should go further and even extend its duty of care to helping people to enjoy the freedom to practice the religion of their choice. The state can play an important role in preventing political interventions in the name of religion.

I am sad to have to say that these principles have taken quite a beating in India. Recently several states within India have prohibited one kind of religious practice or another, including the prohibition of particular types of food. An example is beef by members of one community. Similarly inter-religious marriage has been put under cessation and sometimes even under prohibition, in spite of the fact that there is no prohibition on the chosen religions of couples who desire to marry. Also, there are stories of forcible religious conversion of the bride, particularly in newspapers. But, as court cases have tended to show again and again, these accusations are often very hard to support with evidence.

The concept of secularism was discussed long before Bangabandhu by the Mughal Emperor Akbar towards the end of the 16th century. He came to the conclusion that there should not be any ban on religious practice freely chosen by the people. The state should help in preserving this freedom, but no religion should enjoy privileges that might disadvantage another religion.

There are then, here, two contrasting versions of secularism. One is the resistance to religious imbalance or asymmetry as emphasized by Akbar. The other is the focus on resisting the use of religion for political gain. It was on this that Bangabandhu focused. The two versions are similar but different. But the abuse of either one is a violation that has a similar effect in going against the religious freedom of the people.

The understanding of secularism as explained by Sheikh Mujib and by the Emperor Akbar is particularly important internationally today. It clearly applies ever more so in India, but also in other countries across the globe. The matter remains relevant to political discussions also in the United States and Europe, often not directly in the form of religion, but when it comes to similar acts of discrimination such as race or ethnic asymmetry.

In the subcontinent, the news often touches on issues such as unrest in Pakistan and Sri Lanka. But the Indian situation is perhaps more troubling when it is taken in its historical perspective – until recently, and for many decades, India was much closer to practicing secular democracy.

As mentioned, the *Bangabandhu* title recognised Sheikh Mujib as a friend of Bengal but he can also be referred to as as *Bishobandhu* – a friend of the world. The impact of his thinking, and the spread of his ideas, have carried influence far beyond his homeland or native continent. They have spread across the world. Sheikh Mujib saw secularism in the context of personal freedom and it was a subject on which his focus remained strong and steady.

Another important freedom was linguistic. One of Bangabandhu's central concerns was about the use of one's mother tongue, in the fight for which he prooved leadership. He made clear that it was central to the very concept of the Bengali nation and was linked closely with the individual's freedom to use his or her own language.

This is a subject that also generates much interst elsewhere in subcontinental discussions. An example is the importance given to the Sinhalese as opposed to the Tamils in Sri Lanka. It is possible that Sri Lanka might have escaped war and much bloodshed had the political leaders of the country paid more attention to Sheikh Mujib's analysis of languagesissues and had they understood the need to make room for people's mother language.

The wisdom of Bangabandhu's social analysis on language use and application goes far beyond Bengal. We are establishing the status of languages for all the major languages in India – something the importance of which started to be recognised quite early in the history of Indian policy. Had there been a greater focus earlier, some serious problems could surely have been avoided quite early in the development of modern India. There are contrasts in the privileges enjoyed by those on one side whose mother tongue happens to be Hindi, or in some cases English, versus those who speak a different mother tongue. The possible inequality of language may deserve more attention than it tends to get. This may be, to some extent, an issue in West Bengal as well – a multi-lingual region with a range of languages spoken.

Last but not least in a this brief examination of Bangabandhu's concerns is the importance of increasing equality between people. In seeking independence from undivided Pakistan, his egalitarian concepts played a significant role, and indeed were central to much of the thinking of the Awami League he led. In the campaign speeches for the crucially important 1970 general election, Bangabandhu did not hesitate to place the issue of equity between different religious communities in the forefront. It was a brave move, bearing in mind an unpredictable voting public divided between Muslims and Hindus. Nonetheless he insisted on the principle that:

> *"The people of the minority community are entitled to enjoy equal rights and opportunities, like any other citizen."*

Despite the fact that East Pakistan has a largely Muslim majority population, the egalitarian sentiment seeking justice for the minority community did not interfere with the spectacular election success because Bangabandhu was highly persuasive in arguing his point on this case. As it turned out, the Awami League got 167 out of 169 seats allocated to East Pakistan in the National Assembly in that election of 1970. It was an illustration of the effectiveness of his golden reasoning and one that was to be repeated in many other episodes in Sheikh Mujib's life and politics. But underpinning his persuasiveness is the central point that he did not hesitate to present and defend on the basis of what he considered right, not on what he judged politically expedient.

To conclude, we must never forget how Bangabandhu frequently navigated his political actions on the basis of moral principle tempered with a respect for traditional values in Bengal. Bangabandhu's egalitarian concern can be traced back to ancient poetry, reflecting the views of socially conscious poets such as Kazi Nazrul Islam. Even the very earliest Bengali poetry tended to focus on this theme. The earliest Bengali poets, writing in an ancient form of the Bengali language, often revealed their concern for the importance of equality. Let me give an example. When Bengali was evolving, one of the earliest scripts was what is called Charjapod. The devoted poet Shidwacharja Bushuku reflected in Charjapod, in early 10th century Bengali on his river journey as he was carried from the West of Bengal through to the East of Bengal. On the way East, a range of adventures befell Shidwacharja – he was robbed of his property by pirates and he married a woman of the lowest stratum of the society, a woman of the Chandal caste. So, Shidwacharja offered the following poem. In its an English translation, it goes:

> *"I have steered thunderbolts along the course of the River Padma. The pirates have robbed me of my misery. Bushuku, today, you have become true Bengali by having taken a Chandal woman as your wife."*

We have to understand that what they meant by 'being Bengali' was not in those days being resident anywhere in Bengal, but it referred to being some one from what we now call Dhaka and Faridpur. That was what it meant to be Bengali, and, we can see that the "two Bangalis" were in existence many thousands of years ago.

As it happened, Bangabandhu was born in Tungipara, in Dhaka. Since I too am from Dhaka as well I have to cultivate my courage before ending this talk to greet an exceptional neighbour whose great ideas and leadership certainly, I say with pride, 'changed the world'.

Thank you.

Amartya Sen
January 2021

THE STORIES

*The best people renounce all
for one goal*

Heraclitus
(c. 535 – c. 475 BCE)

i

Sheikh Mujib was always grateful to Huseyn Shaheed Suhrawardy for kick-starting his political career. Regardless, even Suhrawardy was not allowed to humiliate Mujib without repercussions.

In 1944, during the All-Bengal Muslim Chhatra League annual meeting, opportunists were trying to take advantage of Suhrawardy's generosity for their personal political gain. As Mujib tried to advise him on the issue, Suhrawardy exclaimed, "Who are you? You are nobody." The twenty-two year old Sheikh Mujib looked his mentor straight in the eye and replied, "If I am nobody, then why have you invited me? You have no right to insult me. I will prove that I am somebody. Thank you Sir. I will never come to you again."

Mujib stormed out of the meeting, leaving behind a shocked Suhrawardy.

ii

During the Muslim League's "Direct Action Day" on 16 August 1946, communal riots spread like wildfire in Kolkata, Noakhali, Dhaka and Bihar. Hindus were attacked and slaughtered in Noakhali, while Muslims suffered the same fate in Bihar. Sheikh Mujib hurried to Bihar acting on Suhrawardi's instruction and jumped straight into action outright to help people regardless of their differing faiths. Suhrawardy made a plan to relocate the victims of the Bihar riots to Asansol, where the provincial government of Bengal could rehabilitate them. Mujib was closely affiliated with the rehabilitation process.

He and his coworkers did not have any special food arrangements for themselves during this time; they ate the same food as the refugees, and never had more than one meal a day. Almost all of Mujib's group of volunteers, including himself, fell ill due to lack of food and sleep. When Muslim League leaders came to supervise the refugee camps, they were shocked to see Mujib's haggard appearance. With their persuasion, Mujib returned to Kolkata following one and a half months of volunteer work.

iii

"Mr Hashim was a follower of Maulana Azad Sobhani, a reputed philosopher. Mr Hashim invited him to Kolkata. He would teach classes there. My colleagues would listen to his lectures till late into the night. It was tough for me to sit still patiently. I would escape after attending the lectures for some time. I told my friends, 'You all go and become scholars. I have too much that needs to be done. First we have to create Pakistan, then we will have time for intellectual discussions.'

Mr Hashim had poor vision, fortunately for me. But he knew that I would sneak out from the back of the class. The next day, he would say, 'Hey, you went off last night.' I would reply, 'What can I say, I had too much work to do.'

Throughout I kept up engagements with the students. I needed to maintain the Party."

iv

Mujib was arrested by the Pakistani government at the end of 1949 for his involvement in the Language Movement. He was held in captivity as a political prisoner for two years and five months, being repeatedly transferred between jails in Dhaka, Faridpur and Khulna. The plight of imprisonment had taken a toll on him, and he fell seriously ill. On 25 February, a civil surgeon came to inspect him and was alarmed at his frail state. "What use will it be to die like this?" the surgeon asked. "You are the hope of Bangladesh."

Mujib replied, "There are many others left. My work will not be left undone. I love my country and my people - I am content to sacrifice my life for them."

V

In 1950, communal riots began in Kolkata and Dhaka over rumours that Sher-e-Bangla had been killed by Hindus. Many innocent Muslims in Kolkata, and Hindus in Dhaka and Barishal lost their lives in these riots. Mujib was then in jail for the third time. He spoke to the arrested ordinary people, discouraging communal violence and explaining that Islam discouraged violence and hatred towards all human beings. Mujib met Mr. Chandra Ghosh from Gopalganj when he was transferred to Faridpur Jail. Mr. Chandra Ghosh was a humanitarian and social worker respected by both Hindus and Muslims. Yet, he was imprisoned by the fundamentalist Pakistan government. On his deathbed, Mr. Chandra Ghosh took Mujib's hand and implored him to look past people's religious differences and view them all as human beings. Mujib dried his tears and replied,

"Do not worry, I see humans only as humans. There are no Muslims, Hindus or Christians in my politics. Everyone is human."

vi

When Mujib returned to his home in 1952 after being imprisoned for more than two years, he overheard his son Sheikh Kamal - who had only been a few months old when he was sent to jail - ask his daughter Sheikh Hasina, "Hasu Apa, let me call your father Abba too." Mujib, holding back tears, picked his son up and said, "But I am your father too."

He spent so much of his political career in prison that his eldest daughter, Sheikh Hasina, rarely had an opportunity to spend time with her father during her childhood. The loss of this irreplaceable experience of fatherhood was particularly painful for Mujib. It was this sacrifice of countless precious memories with his loved ones for the sake of his cause, and his devotion to his countrymen, that earned him the titles of "Bangabandu" - the friend of Bengal, and the "Father of the Nation."

vii

In 1952, on a tour in China, Mujib visited an ordinary home, with a view to witnessing the results of China's socialist revolution. Only a newly-wed housewife was present there. Mujib thought that it had been impolite to arrive at the house empty-handed, and would reflect poorly on his country's image. Unable to find anything else, he took off his own ring and presented it to his host. He explained, "In my country the custom is to bring a gift whenever you visit a newly-wed couple's home."[1]

---

1   From *China As I Saw It*, Sheikh Mujibur Rahman.

viii

"In early 1953, I [Obaidul Huq] was with several Awami League leaders including Mawlana Abdul Hamid Khan Bhasani and Sheikh Mujibur Rahman, returning to Bhola from Barishal. Mawlana Bhashani went to sleep and some of us including Miya Bhai[Mujib] were chatting on the hood of the boat and one of us said, "If we could induce an armed revolution like Masterda Surya Sen did, we probably could shake off the clasp of the Punjabis."

Miya Bhai retorted, "Three decades after the armed revolution led by Masterda Surya Sen, the situation is far more volatile now; hence another armed revolution is out of question in this new era. Our movement is taking a democratic approach, and the paramount priority has to be put on encouraging the mass people."

"Then Miya Bhai urged us to keep silent and listen to the people returning home from the market, as they were venting their frustration at the deteriorating condition of the country and its impact on their personal lives. Miya Bhai said to us, "People are getting conscious nowadays; I see a glimpse of a dream waiting to be achieved in what I hear."

ix

Mujib visited many villages in Gopalganj while campaigning for the United Front during the 1954 election. He came into close contact with the voters in these villages. On one of his campaign visits, an elderly woman stood by the road for hours to see him. She held his hand and invited him to her tiny hut, where she offered him milk, betel leaf and a few coins. "Please eat and take this money, my son," she said, "I have nothing else to offer." Mujib teared up at her words. He took a sip of the milk and then offered her some of his own money alongside the coins she had given him. "Your blessings are more than enough for me. No amount of money can be more valuable than that." The old woman refused to take the money. She stroked his head and face, and said, "The blessings of the poor are with you." Mujib began to cry when he was leaving her hut.

He wrote in his memoir, "Before the 1954 election, I had no idea how much the people of this country love me."

x

In 1966, before flying to the Soviet Union to sign a peace treaty with India, Ayub Khan wished to improve his image in front of the foreign media by arranging negotiations with the leaders of East Pakistan. The Ayub administration invited Bengali leaders to meet with Monem Khan, the then appointed governor of East Pakistan. While some of these leaders accepted the invitation, Mujib insisted that he would only talk to Ayub himself. Ayub Khan was aware of Sheikh Mujibur Rahman's political significance in East Pakistan, so he arranged a meeting in Dhaka on 25 December 1965. Five representatives of the Awami League, including Mujib and Tajuddin Ahmed, were in attendance.

Ayub began the meeting by displaying his characteristic careless arrogance, saying, "So why are you here, what do you wish to say?"

Mujib immediately stood up and retorted, "None of us have come here by himself, you have invited us. You may be this country's President but you have no right to invite us here and then humiliate us."

This champion's courage came from the love of his countrymen and his unbreakable sense of self-respect.

xi

The Awami League won the majority of seats in the national election of 1970, but president Yahya Khan stalled the formal inauguration. On 2 March 1971, Sheikh Mujib called for a peaceful non-cooperative resistance in Dhaka and 3 March across East Pakistan with nationwide boycotts and communication block-off, while holding formal negotiations with Yahya. While announcing his plans for the non-cooperative movement, Mujib repeatedly warned protesters to avoid engaging in extremist violence. "We are a democratic party that believes in democratic methods," he explained. "We will carry out a peaceful and organized resistance."

"I call on the people to observe the strike in a disciplined and peaceful way, and to keep watch for unwanted incidents, such as looting and arson."

"Mujib's non-cooperation movement extended from 3 March to 25 March and was organized and controlled." NAP leader Wali Khan witnessed the success of the movement and commented, "Even (Mahatma) Gandhi would have marvelled."

xii

On the night of 25 March 1971, the Pakistani army commenced "Operation Searchlight", the beginning of a nine-months long genocide. Mujib declared independence of Bangladesh in the early hours of 26 March 1971. His message was clear:

> *"This may be my last message; from this day onward Bangladesh is independent. I call upon the people of Bangladesh wherever you might be and with whatever you have, to resist the army of occupation to the last. Your struggle must go on until the last soldier of the Pakistan occupation army is expelled from the soil of Bangladesh. Final victory is ours."*

On 17 April 1971, elected representatives of 1970's election, formed the government-in-exile for the 'People's Republic of Bangladesh'. In the proclamation of independence, Sheikh Mujibur Rahman was promulgated as the in-absentia president of Bangladesh. 'Joy Bangla' and 'Joy Bangabandhu' were the motto of hope for the freedom fighters.

In August 1971, the Pakistani regime put imprisoned Mujib on a farcical trial and was sentenced to death. On December 16, 1971, ninety-three thousand

soldiers of the defeated Pakistan army along with their commanders surrendered at the racecourse ground in Dhaka. Bangladesh emerged as a newly independent country on the world map.

Due to the pressure put by the international community, the Pakistani government had no choice but to release Mujib. He returned to sovereign Bangladesh after 9 months and 14 days of imprisonment. His journey back to home had two stopovers, first in London, where he was warmly welcomed by British Prime Minister Edward Heath, and then to Delhi and on to Dhaka, two centers which mobilized the opinion at global level for the independence of Bangladesh and also the seats of the closest allies.

xiii

In 1973, Mujib attended the conference of the Non-Alignment Movement at Algiers, Algeria, where he met the Cuban revolutionary leader Fidel Castro. Embracing Bangabandhu Sheikh Mujibur Rahman, Castro remarked: "I have not seen the Himalayas. But I have seen Sheikh Mujib. In personality and in courage, this man is the Himalayas. I have thus had the experience of witnessing the Himalayas."

In the conference, Mujib met Libyan head of state Colonel Gaddafi and asked him to formally acknowledge Bangladesh as an independent state.

In reply, Gaddafi demanded that Mujib rename his country the "Islamic Republic of Bangladesh."

"But that is not possible," Mujib calmly answered, "Bangladesh is everyone's country — both Muslim and non-Muslim."

xiv

Mujib was at Pabna campaigning for the election in 1973. As he was speaking to some local leaders before the meeting began, he suddenly became very concerned, and surprised everyone by shouting out and hurrying to the entrance of the venue. Some event volunteers had been pushing a group of little boys from the village away from the entrance of the venue, and one of the boys was injured. Mujib berated the volunteers, comforted the children and ordered the volunteers to never mistreat children in such a way again. He could not tolerate an act of class discrimination and injustice, especially against helpless children.

xv

As the supreme leader of the country from 1972 to 1975, Sheikh Mujib had every opportunity to abuse his power against the perpetrators of war crimes, but he instead chose to display his pacifist nature to avoid any instability and disruption to the development process of the country. In this he showed fair judgement and accountability.

When Shah Azizur Rahman and Sabur Khan – both Pakistan supporters and Mujib's political rivals – were imprisoned for their war crimes, Mujib took the time to check on their families.

When others criticized his actions he responded, "Those who committed the crimes are being brought to justice. Why should others suffer?"

He treated Abdul Matin – a leader of the East Bengal Communist Party – with honour and dignity as he sought for Mujib's custody, despite the fact that Matin had announced plans to violently overthrow the Mujib regime.

xvi

In 1974, a devastating famine occurred as the country was swept by a massive flood. At the same time, the United States of America withheld a crucial shipment of food to Bangladesh.

Mujib personally visited several countries, desperately seeking aid. He set up more than five thousand free food centres. Despite his efforts, the famine claimed 27,000 lives. According to Nurul Islam, then deputy chair of the Bangladesh Planning Commission, Mujib was extremely depressed during this period and never ate more than one meal a day; and he refused to eat rice. When approached regarding this issue, he exclaimed, "By what right will I have rice when my people can't!"

xvii

During the devastating famine of 1974, Mujib had to visit New York to attend the UN's general meeting as a new member. Mujib was furious at the USA's role in the famine, and also resented the US Secretary of State Henry Kissinger for his remark in an interview a few days earlier in which he called Bangladesh 'an international basket case'. Kissinger had opposed the independence of Bangladesh in 1971 as well.

Mujib shot back at Kissinger in a press conference in Washington D.C., saying, "Some consider Bangladesh an international basket case, some mock us. But Bangladesh is not a basket case. Our resources have been looted for two hundred years. Our resources have been used to build London, Dundee, Manchester, Karachi and Islamabad. Even today Bangladesh has unlimited resources. One day we will show the world how Bangladesh has stood up on its own."

Kissinger himself visited Bangladesh later on October 29. Speaking about Mujib, he sayd: "A Man of vast conception. I had rarely met a man who was the father of his nation and this was a particularly unique experience for me."

WORDS

History is Philosophy teaching by examples.

Thucydides
(c. 460 – c. 400 BCE)

HUMANISM & IDEOLOGY

"As a man, what concerns mankind concerns me. As a Bangali, I am deeply involved in all that concerns Bangalis. This abiding involvement is born of and nourished by love, enduring love, which gives meaning to my politics and to my very being."

May 30, 1973

THE INDOMINATABLE SPIRIT OF MANKIND

"I would like to conclude by reaffirming my faith in the indomitable spirit of man – in the capacity of the people to act even the impossible and to overcome insurmountable odds. This is the faith which sustains nations like us which have emerged through struggle and sacrifice. Our nations may suffer, but they can never die. In facing the challenge of survival, the resilience and determination of the people is an ultimate strength."

UN General Assembley , New York, USA,
September 25, 1975

ON NATURE

"When I start strolling around the garden in the morning, the struggles of the night don't cross my mind anymore. I sit on a chair under a tree and dive into a newspaper or a book. The morning breeze takes away all the sorrows and sufferings off of my mind. Every day at around 10-11 am, two orioles fly to the mango tree close to my quarter. I watch them play. I think I've fallen in love with them. Two other orioles used to come here in 1958. The two birds that are here now in their stead seem a little bit smaller.

When I came back this time, I started looking for them as soon as I recalled. Even then, I found two orioles here, descendants of those two, I think.

Seems like they either have died or have gone away elsewhere. I automatically start thinking about them by 10-11 am. I haven't been seeing them for quite a few days. I look for them every day. Have they forsaken me? Will I not see them ever again? I will be hurt beyond words if they don't come back."

The Prison Diaries, Sheikh Mujibur Rahman

BENGALI NATIONALISM & BEYOND

"The word 'Bengal' has a history, has a tradition of its own. If you want to change it, then we will have to go back to Bengal and ask them whether they accept it."
Pakistan General Assembly, October, 1958

"Today, the people of Bangla want freedom, they want to survive, they demand their rights."

Suhrawardi Udyan, March 7, 1971

"Those of you who do not speak Bengali, you are now the people of Bengal. You are also our brethren. We need to show the world that Bengalis can not only sacrifice their lives for independence, but also live in peace."

Official inauguration as Prime Minister, January 10, 1972

"A beggar nation has no dignity. When a nation has to beg for food and money, it can never be respectable. I do not want to lead a beggar nation."

Suhrawardi Udyan, March 26, 1975

"If someone has no home, you should put in effort to make one. If someone has no food, you should eat a meal and donate the other. That is humanity. That is brotherhood."

May 9, 1972

ON SECULARISM

"There are two sides to us Bangalis - 'we are Muslims' and 'we are Bangalis'. Envy and treachery run through our veins... Here, brothers are not happy to see their brothers succeed. Despite so much potential, Bengalis have had to face so much oppression for generations due to their own flaws. They do not know themselves, and will not be free until they do."

The Unfinished Memoirs, Sheikh Mujibur Rahman

ON SOCIAL JUSTICE

"The struggle continues against corrupt and unlawful governance, military suppression of people's democratic rights, racism and discrimination. We must take a firm stand against these, for they are human rights violations."

United Nations General Assembly,
September 25, 1974

"We want to build a society free from oppression, and a socialist economy. Our economic system will take into account our culture, our backgrounds, our people and our resources."

On BKSL,
June 19, 1975

DEFINING DEMOCRACY

"If a leader asks for something unjust, the people have the right to protest against him and explain the problem."

In criticism of Jinnah's declaration of Urdu
as the state language, 1948

"I said, if a single person says something rightful, we will heed to him, in spite of being the majority."

Suhrawardy Udyan,
March 7, 1971

"Those who think they can create a revolution out of terrorist activities like gunfights and rail destruction don't even know where they are. This technique has existed for a very long time, yet has failed to achieve anything anywhere in the world."

Awami League's bi-annual conference,
January 18, 1974

ON DUTY

"I am speaking to you not as your president or leader, but as your brother. Rebuild the devastated Bangladesh into a happy and resourceful country. Start building your own roads. Do your jobs. We cannot let anyone else die of hunger. We cannot allow any more bribery and corruption."

On return to homeland,
January 10, 1972

"I will say this to our educated society – your character has not changed at all. Those poor farmers and laborers provide your salaries. Those people you look down upon are like your fathers and brothers. They work harder than you, so they deserve more respect."

Suhrawardy Udyan,
March 16, 1975

"We cannot purify if we do not evaluate. If we do

not learn from our mistakes, and always think ourselves right and everyone else wrong – now that is just absurd. Whenever I make a mistake, I must remember that I can rectify myself. If I can rectify my mistake, then I am successful."

First BKSL core committee meeting,
June 19, 1975

ACTIONS

What you leave behind is not what is engraved in stone monuments, but what is woven into the lives of others.

Pericles
(c. 495 – c. 429 BCE)

THE BATTLE AGAINST COMMUNISM

Mujib was part of the progressive wing of the
Muslim League. He campaigned for the party
with a view to ensuring the political and economic
rights of British India's minority Muslims. He began
to admire Rabindranath Tagore, Chittaranjan
Das and Subhas Bose for speaking out against the
exploitation of poor Muslims by Hindu upper-caste
landowners and moneylenders.

He played a vital role in mitigating the communal
violence of 1946 and 1950 fanned by the reactionary
faction of the Muslim League and the Hindu
Mahasabha. He risked his life to protect victims of
the riots regardless of different faiths.

After the Muslim-majority state of Pakistan was
established in 1947, Mujib and his co-workers
proposed to form a new cultural organization called
the 'Ganatantrik Jubo League', aimed at promoting
interfaith unity and discouraging communal violence.

On June 24, 1949, the progressive wing of the
Muslim League formed the 'East Pakistan Awami
Muslim League', with Maulana Bhashani as the
chair. Young Mujib also left the increasingly power
hungry Muslim League, sickened with fellow
members' corrupt practice for political power. He
was appointed as the general secretary of the new
party in 1953.

On October 23, 1955, two years after Mujib became
general secretary, the party was renamed the 'East
Pakistan Awami League.' This monumental decision
made the party a representative of voters from all
faiths across East Pakistan. Under his leadership,
the Awami League embraced secularism as a core

principle, resisting the reactionary Muslim League administration.

In 1964, following the death of Suhrawardy, many senior politicians left the party. Through resilient and pragmatic approach, Mujib succeeded in maintaining and strengthening his group and retaining its general members.

On January 16, 1964, he formed the 'Danga Pratirodh Committee' with ninety-nine influential Dhaka citizens, encouraging the citizens of East Pakistan to promote interfaith harmony and protect their minority brothers and sisters from intolerance. Mujib and his colleague Tajuddin Ahmed were arrested on the charge of defaming the military government.

LANGUAGE AT THE HEART

In 1947, when the Muslim League formed a government with Khwaja Nazimuddin as the Governor General, the 22-year-old Mujib refused to submit to the communalist propaganda of reactionary politicians and mobilized the mass people to resist the government's oppressive tactics. Following the government's decision to proclaim Urdu as the only state language, Mujib's East Pakistan Muslim Student League collaborated with the cultural organization Tamaddun Majlish to organize the 'Rashtrabhasha Bangla Sangram Parishad'.

On 11 March 1948, the police began beating up protesters observing the 'Bangla Bhasha Dabi Dibash' indiscriminately and Mujib was imprisoned by the central Pakistani government for the very first time. On 19 March, Governor General Muhammad

Ali Jinnah visited Dhaka to repeat that Urdu would be the state language. Mujib continued to speak out against the decision, bravely criticizing Jinnah. Around the same time, a new political party called the East Pakistan Muslim Awami League was formed while he was imprisoned from March 11 to 15, and he was named the Joint Secretary.

Immediately after he was released, he began organizing the new party. He had to violate Section 144 – a law that punished public gatherings of more than five people – in order to form the party and hold meetings. He refused to be subdued even after the government sent goons and the police after him. He never tried to evade any of his many arrests, rather strongly proclaimed,, "I do not do politics in secret. I do politics for the people and will go to jail in front of the people."

In early 1952, the Bangla Language Movement livened up again, as Khwaja Nazimuddin disregarded his previous agreement and announced Urdu as the only state language. Imprisoned Mujib arranged secret meetings with political and student leaders in the hospital balcony. He, along with Mohiuddin Ahmed, a student leader from Barisal and a fellow political prisoner, declared a hunger strike from February 16 to protest the proclamation of Urdu as the state language, as well as the economic exploitation of East Bengal, and the fact that he had been a political prisoner for more than two years. Despite the Faridpur jail authority's many attempts, including forcing food down their throats with nozzles, they refused to eat anything except saline water.

A CHARTER FOR JUSTICE

The Six Point Movement of 1966 highlighted Mujib's desire for economic, political and cultural freedom of Bangladesh, and his ultimate vision - combining socialism with democracy and Bangali nationalism for a truly equitable society. He originally presented this manifesto at a national conference in Lahore in February 1966, which was criticized and rejected by West Pakistani politicians, news media, and non-Awami League politicians from East Pakistan. On February 11, he flew back to Dhaka and announced his decision for the Six Point Movement to the press at the airport. Mujib's six demands were published in flyers and distributed across East Pakistan.

The six points are as follows:

1. The Constitution should provide for a Federation of Pakistan in its true sense based on the Lahore Resolution, and the parliamentary form of government with supremacy of a Legislature directly elected on the basis of universal adult franchise.

2. The federal government should deal with only two subjects: Defence and Foreign Affairs, and all other residual subjects should be vested in the federating states.

3. Two separate, but freely convertible currencies for two wings should be introduced; or if this is not feasible, there should be one currency for the whole country, but effective constitutional provisions should be introduced to stop the flight of capital from East to West Pakistan. Furthermore, a separate Banking

Reserve should be established and separate fiscal and monetary policy be adopted for East Pakistan.

4. The power of taxation and revenue collection should be vested in the federating units and the federal centre would have no such power. The federation would be entitled to a share in the state taxes to meet expenditures.

5. There should be two separate accounts for the foreign exchange earnings of the two wings; the foreign exchange requirements of the federal government should be met by the two wings equally or in a ratio to be fixed; indigenous products should move free of duty between the two wings, and the constitution should empower the units to establish trade links with foreign countries.

6. East Pakistan should have a separate military or paramilitary force, and the Navy headquarters should be in East Pakistan.

ELECTION '70: THE MANDATE

In 1964, the military dictator General Ayub Khan declared an election based on his 'basic democracy' system (80,000 representative voters would elect the president as well as the members of parliament, while the general population lost their democratic right) to be held in January 1965. The Awami League, the National Awami Party, Jamaat-e-Islami, Council Muslim League and Nizam-e-Islami formed a coalition and nominated a single candidate for the presidential election. Mujib was unsurprised by Ayub

Khan's victory – he knew that 'basic democracy' was an exploitative and unfair ploy. By participating in this election, however, he clearly demonstrated the unfairness of the system to mass people.

In 1966, Mujib spearheaded the legendary Six Point Movement, which called for greater autonomy for East Pakistan. As Mujib continued to mobilize the people of East Pakistan to stand up for their rights, Ayub Khan began a desperate crackdown as an attempt to antagonize Mujib's mass popularity, and arrested him again. Following a public upsurge known as the Mass Revolution of 1969, Mujib was released from jail, and sat down for a new round of negotiations with Ayub, in which Ayub agreed to restore general elections and parliamentary democracy.

However, on March 25, 1969, Ayub Khan was overthrown in a military coup by General Yahya Khan, killing all hope for further progress; consequently pulsating an increasingly anti-government ideology among the general Bangalis. Extremist groups took advantage of this situation and tried to distort the independence movement with boycotts, fires, and violent strikes. Sheikh Mujib urged his countrymen to resist surges of violence and participate in a peaceful and organized movement for democracy. Following his call, the situation calmed down significantly.

Instead of submitting the mantle, Mujib now turned his attentions towards the election of 1970. During the electoral campaigns, the Awami League promised the Bangali voter base that an Awami League government would try to establish a socialist economy, establish a constitutional administration, nationalize major industries and increase

71

opportunities for landless farmers.

The Awami League won 167 out of 169 of East Pakistan (313 seats in total) in the 1970 Pakistan elections, and won the mandate to form the government. But as president Yahya kept stalling the formal inauguration, Mujib called for a peaceful non-cooperative resistance across East Pakistan on March 3, 1971.

STRUGGLE FOR FREEDOM

As a lifelong advocate of peace, Sheikh Mujib primarily worked for twenty-four years to achieve the independence of Bangladesh without bloodshed, through negotiation and a well-organized non-cooperation movement. The call for movement on March 7, 1971 was a final ultimatum for the Pakistani military junta, and the Declaration of Independence came as a response of the massacre in East Pakistan, codenamed 'Operation Searchlight' on March 25, 1972. Mujib was arrested as a part of this operation. His constitutional method of politics allowed him to prioritize the security of the Bangali people as much as possible, legitimize Bangladeshi independence movement to the rest of the world, and build the foundation for a lawful future of Bangladesh.

The Liberation War itself was carried out systematically, Mujib having laid down the precise framework. In Mujib's absence, Tajuddin Ahmed and Syed Nazrul Islam organized their efforts in a disciplined and efficient way. In 1970, Mujib had recruited two Bangali officers retired from the Pakistani army – Bangabir Colonel Osmani and Bir Uttam Colonel Abdul Rab – into the Awami League, and instructed his party members on obtaining shelter in India.

While Mujib was in jail, these leaders were able to compile the announcement of independence charter within merely two weeks after the massacre of March 25. In addition, both the commander and vice-commander of the Liberation War were elected parliament members from the Awami League. None of these facts were coincidences. Mujib's actions and precautions revealed his pragmatic nature, and established the Liberation War as a completely constitutional and systematic decision by a fair, democratically elected government.

He was imprisoned in Pakistan for the entirety of the Liberation War, while his family was placed under house arrest in Dhaka. While Mujib was in prison, the Pakistani government attempted coercion tactics to make him surrender and call off the guerrilla war. The prison administration had dug a grave beside his prison cell and frequently threatened to execute him. Bhutto personally visited Mujib and offered a position in his cabinet, Mujib merely smirked at the attempt.

Mujib finally returned to his beloved country on January 10, 1972. The very day after his return, he announced his decision to introduce a new parliamentary system.

FROM THE ASHES

Mujib was released from prison in January 1972 and visited India instead while returning to his country. Indian Prime Minister Indira Gandhi herself welcomed him at the Delhi airport. Mujib promptly took the opportunity to express his gratitude towards Mrs Gandhi and the Indian populace for their support and hospitality towards Bangladeshi refugees and freedom fighters. He also carefully ensured that India's relationship with the war-torn, poverty-ridden Bangladesh did not result in a power imbalance, and made Mrs Gandhi vow to withdraw Indian soldiers as soon as possible. He recognized that having foreign soldiers posted in an independent country projected an image of instability. Mujib wished for independent Bangladesh to have a dignified image from the very beginning.

On January 10, 1972, Mujib returned to an independent Bangladesh, after spending months imprisoned in Pakistan during the war. Instead of resting and recovering from physical and mental trauma, he dived straight into the monumental task of restoring and building up the country he cherished by heart.

On March 25, 1972, to commemorate the first anniversary of independence, the Mujib-led government passed laws to nationalize 80 to 84 percent of the manufacturing, banking and insurance industries. The goal was to combat inadequate labor rights and increase production opportunities. He implemented laws to fairly distribute arable land among farmers, and set appropriate punishments for violation of these laws. Mujib also made sure that the laborers in tea gardens obtained Bangladeshi citizenship and voting rights.

On May 3, 1973, the World Peace Committee honoured Sheikh Mujib's contribution to world peace with their highest recognition, the Julio Curie Prize.

POST-WAR RESIDUE

After Mujib became the Prime Minister of independent Bangladesh on January 12, 1972, he announced general amnesty for Bangladeshis who have supported Pakistan during the war, but it excluded culprits guilty of war crimes, such as murder and rape, torture, looting or using firearms.

He arranged for the rehabilitation of more than two hundred thousand rape victims ostracized from society, and sometimes even from their families. Mujib honoured them with the title 'Birangana' – the War Heroines – and announced that they could write down his name and address instead of their fathers' whenever they needed to.

On January 17, 1972, he instructed all civilian freedom fighters to surrender weapons within ten days. He showed respect and gratitude to the freedom fighters, and also made it clear that any weapon remaining after ten days would be considered illegal. He also announced his scheme to assign freedom fighters in different law enforcement, security and development-oriented occupations based on their qualifications. This was his strategy to bring the freedom fighters into order and ensure security for the nation.

On January 22, he extended the deadline to the end of the month. Finally, the ceremony officially ended on January 31 in the Dhaka Stadium.

Alongside his attempt to keep 70 million people satisfied in a war-torn and impoverished country amidst numerous challenges and obstacles, he made a steady progress in rebuilding the country and ensuring the maximum safety for the citizens with minimal resources.

The Daily Welt of Germany published the following report on December 8, 1972:

> *"In Dhaka, Chittagong or Comilla, pedestrians can feel secure walking down the streets even at night. The streets in these cities are not particularly unsafe in comparison with Frankfurt's or New York's. The reason behind such an incredible accomplishment is Mujib. He is the binding force of the state."*

PART OF THE WORLD COMMUNITY

On March 26, 1972, Mujib addressed the country on the occasion of Bangladesh's first Independence Day, and revealed his impartial stance on international politics. He announced that Bangladesh's approach to foreign politics was to be non-interventionist, and focused on developing positive relations with all its neighbours. During the Cold War, Bangladesh remained neutral and joined the Non-Aligned Movement.

In 1974, Bangladesh joined the second OIC summit as per request of the leaders of several Muslim countries, with the pretext that Pakistan must recognize Bangladesh as a sovereign country. It was a brilliant strategy by Sheikh Mujib to gain the recognition of Bangladesh from the enemy of the war, which would project a complete manifesto of the victory for Bangladesh. Finally, Pakistan gave Bangladesh official recognition on February 22, 1979. Bangladesh attained recognition from a total of 116 countries with Mujib's sheer effort and diplomatic charisma.

After Bangladesh became a member of the United Nations, Mujib delivered a historic speech in Bangla at the UN headquarters on September 25, 1974, that appealed to pacifists around the world.

THE SECOND REVOLUTION

Mujib's vision for Bangladesh repeatedly surfaced throughout the whole timeline of the struggle for freedom. The proclamation of independence published on April 10, 1971 clearly stated that the objective was to ensure equality, respect and legal rights for the people of Bangladesh. It strongly identified nationalism, socialism, democracy and secularism as the state's core values.

The BKSL initiative, which Mujib called his 'Second Revolution', was a strategy to quickly and selfsufficiently rebuild the country to tackle the aftermath of the 1974 famine, as well as in the context of the extremist violence that had been disrupting the economy.

On March 26, 1975, Mujib commemorated the nation's fifth Independence Day by announcing his decision to build an improvised socialist economic system taking the culture, heritage and resources into account; and called on the people in general to participate in achieving four goals: ending corruption, increasing production in farms and factories, population planning and national unity. The decision did not come through violation of the Constitution, rather by officially introducing an amendment on January 25, 1975.

Cowards die many times before their deaths;
The valiant never taste death but once.

Julius Caesar, Act II, Scene ii,
William Shakespeare

Mujib was a people's leader and, despite being the prime minister, kept his residence accessible always for the public. He stayed at his humble private residence where he would be assassinated in the pre-dawn hours on 15 August 1975. A handful of renegades from the military killed Mujib and almost all of his family members. Each of his closest, with the exception of his two daughters, Sheikh Hasina and Sheikh Rehana, were murdered in one of the most heinous crimes against humanity in contemporary times. The killers were patronized by the vested interests groups who never approved or accepted Bangladesh's emergence as a secular state.

Like many other larger than life leaders – among them Abraham Lincoln, Mahatma Gandhi, Patrice Lumumba, John F. Kennedy, Martin Luther King Jr. – Mujib, too, died defending his ideology to the last breath and continues to remain immortal.